QUILT NATIONAL

❦

CONTEMPORARY DESIGNS IN FABRIC

QUILT NATIONAL

CONTEMPORARY DESIGNS IN FABRIC

Coproduced By Lark Books And
The Dairy Barn Southeastern Cultural Arts Center

Lark Books

Asheville, North Carolina, USA

Front Cover: Detail. Ann Curtis. See page 41.

Page 1: Lynne Heller. See page 85.

Page 3: Detail. Gerry Chase. See page 79.

Published in 1995 by Lark Books
50 College Street
Asheville, North Carolina, 28801, U.S.A.

© 1995 by Altamont Press

Project Director: Hilary Morrow Fletcher
Editor: Dawn Cusick
Art Director: Kathleen Holmes
Photography: Brian Blauser
Production: Elaine Thompson, Kathleen Holmes
Proofreading: Julie Brown

ISBN 0-937274-85-2

Library of Congress Cataloging in Publication Data
Quilt National (1995 : Athens, Ohio)
  Contemporary designs in fabric / Quilt National.
    p.   cm.
  "Coproduced by Lark Books and the Dairy Barn Cultural Arts Center."
  Includes index.
  ISBN 0-937274-85-2
  1. Quilts—United States—History—20th century—Exhibitions.
  2. Quilts—History—20th century—Exhibitions.   I. Dairy Barn
Southeastern Ohio Cultural Arts Center.   II. Title.
NK9112.Q5 .1995
746.46'0973'07477197—dc20   95-6494
                                                             CIP

10 9 8 7 6 5 4 3 2 1

Printed in Hong Kong by Oceanic Graphic Printing

Distributed in the United States by Sterling Publishing
   387 Park Avenue South
   New York, New York 10016

Distributed in Canada by Sterling Publishing,
   c/o Canadian Manda Group, One Atlantic Ave., Suite 105,
   Toronto, Canada M6K 3E7

Distributed in Great Britain and Europe by Cassell PLC,
   Wellington House, 125 Strand, London WC2R 0BB, England

Distributed in Australia by Capricorn Link (Australia) Pty Ltd.,
   P.O. Box 6651, Baulkam Hills, Business Centre, NSW 2153, Australia

The Dairy Barn Southeastern Ohio Cultural Arts Center is thrilled to present Quilt National '95, the ninth biennial international exhibition of art quilts. We are honored and proud to continue the tradition of showcasing the best art quilts being produced in the world today.

This year's exhibition features work by many emerging artists as well as others whose reputations already extend throughout the world. The jury process is designed to protect anonymity and assures access to the exhibition for all artists.

The vision of jurors Ann Batchelder, Libby Lehman, and Linda MacDonald is voiced through the clarity and brilliance of their selections for this collection. We are grateful to them for their commitment to shaping a dynamite show!

I would also like to acknowledge the generosity and support of our sponsors who have made a major commitment to the survival of this project. Quilt National's most special friends include several long-term and continuing sponsors: Fairfield Processing Corporation, Friends of Fiber Art International, the Ohio Arts Council, the City of Athens, and the Athens County Convention and Visitors Bureau. We are particularly grateful for the new sponsorship of Mr. Tadanobu Seto and the Nihon Vogue Company, Ltd. of Tokyo, Japan; for the contribution from the Ohio University Inn; and for the generosity of several private donors. A special thanks also goes to Rob Pulleyn and his staff at Altamont Press for their care and effort in producing this beautiful book.

The Dairy Barn Cultural Arts Center recognizes its responsibility to the public, to those artists who create the Quilt National quilts and also to those whose lives are enriched by viewing them. This is not a responsibility we take lightly. Project Director Hilary Fletcher works throughout the year to assure the success and continuity of each show. Her contributions are valued not only by the Dairy Barn but by the quilt world at large.

And finally, I want to recognize and thank the many volunteers in the Athens community whose assistance is invaluable. They do everything from mailing entry forms to hanging display tags to greeting literally thousands of visitors to repacking the quilts. They make Quilt National possible.

Quilt National is a joy for all of us associated with the Dairy Barn Arts Center and we hope that all our readers and visitors will enjoy it as well.

Susan Cole Urano
Executive Director
Dairy Barn Southeastern Ohio Cultural Arts Center

WHEN THE QUILT NATIONAL PROJECT began in 1979, the founders intended to provide a display forum for quilts that did not necessarily fit within traditional quilt categories, quilts with original block designs instead of reworked traditional patterns, quilts that were more about powerful messages than looking pretty. The majority of these quilts faced frequent rejection by traditional quilt show organizers, and their makers were often considered mavericks in their quilt guilds and communities. The people associated with the newly established Dairy Barn Southeastern Ohio Cultural Arts Center felt strongly, however, that these quilts needed to be seen. Certainly it should be noted that the art quilt was never intended to replace the familiar and functional bedcover in the hearts of the public. Rather, the art quilt is simply a different path; not better, not worse, just different.

Quiltmaking has always been a creative process, and today's art quilts have much in common with quilts from a hundred years ago. Just as antique quilts at one point in time were original, bold, and sometimes controversial creative statements (think of the crazy quilts that fit into no category), today's art quilts are a blending of the artist's life and personal expression. The quiltmaker/artist's response to current influences and situations is what keeps the art form vital.

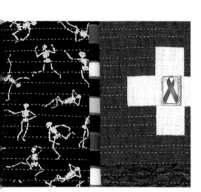

I marvel at the options available to quilters today: the myriad of accessible surface design techniques, nontoxic dyes, revolutions in phototransferring, as well as the commercial availability of hand-dyed fabrics. And yet, is the contemporary quiltmaker's intense interest in making her fabrics truly personal through the use of dyes and surface design techniques really so different from the attachment of quiltmakers in the 1890s to the remnants of a child's christening dress or a grandmother's wedding gown?

Above: Detail. Sara Long. See page 34.

Below: Detail. Jane Dunnewold. See page 40.

Left: Jane Sassaman. See page 104.

As with every Quilt National exhibition, it has been a joy to work with the individual quilts and their respective creators. Unpacking the quilts is like an ongoing Christmas celebration. There is seldom a piece that doesn't pleasantly surprise me — they're almost always so much more interesting and exciting than slide images reveal. Hanging the quilts and playing with how to best light them reveals even more detail. I envy the people who will visit this show and experience the totality of the exhibition. (I know the individual trees too well to recognize the forest as a whole.) I can't help but wonder what people will be thinking as they look at the quilts for the first time. I don't expect them to like each and every quilt, but I do hope they will approach them with open and tolerant minds, and leave them with appreciation and respect for the artists' methods and messages.

I would like to thank the many volunteers who love working with the quilts as much as I do. I would also like to give special thanks to photographer Brian Blauser, whose long-term collaborative efforts have contributed greatly to the success and beauty of the Quilt National books; to Ann Moneypenny for her eager service as a sounding board and for her talents in her official capacity of exhibition designer; and, of course, to Marvin, who makes it possible for me to do a job I love.

Enjoy!

Hilary M. Fletcher
Quilt National Project Director

CONTENTS

Above: Hollis Chatelain. See page 100.

Right: Detail. Sue Benner. See pages 106–107.

10

ANN BATCHELDER has been editor of FIBERARTS Magazine for the past seven years and consulting editor for FIBERARTS Design Books III, IV, and V. She has juried national fiber exhibitions and has been invited to write about fiber art for various books, magazines, and exhibition catalogs. She has a Bachelor's degree in English literature from Kenyon College and a Master's degree from Simmons College Graduate School. Batchelder lives with her husband and two children in the country outside Asheville, North Carolina.

LIBBY LEHMAN is a studio artist who frequently teaches and lectures worldwide. Her quilts are in museum, corporate, and private collections, including the Museum of the American Quilter's Society in Paducah, Kentucky. She is the coauthor of four books, and her work has appeared in many quilt magazines and books. Lehman lives in Houston, Texas, with her husband and son. She has a Bachelor's degree from Rice University and is also a professional calligrapher.

LINDA R. MACDONALD holds a Bachelor's degree in painting and a Master of Fine Arts degree in textiles from San Francisco State University. She has been working in the quilt and fiber field for over 20 years. Her work has been shown extensively, nationally and internationally, and was included in the traveling show "Craft Today U.S.A." Her work is in the permanent collection of the American Craft Museum and in many private collections. She maintains a studio in the small northern California town of Willits and teaches high school art for at-risk students.

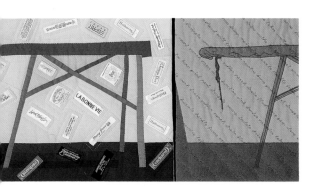

Left: Emily Richardson. See page 98.

Above: Detail. New Image. See page 59.

11

JURORS' STATEMENT

IT WAS A PRIVILEGE and a pleasure to be invited as jurors for the Dairy Barn's 9th Quilt National. This year's exhibition offers what we collectively believe to be the freshest, most innovative, and exciting art work being done today in the quilt medium. Each quilt selected satisfied several criteria in terms of mastery of technique, overall design, and concept. It also had to have clarity and a sense of cohesiveness or completion. In the end, however, a quilt was chosen because it had depth — depth of style, content, technique, or emotion. Something about it made us want to take a second (or third, or fourth) look. Something about it was unique and intriguing.

Each Quilt National exhibition reflects the synergy between three jurors. For us, the jurying process was simultaneously grueling, entertaining, agonizing, and educational. We engaged in hours of lively discussion about the merits of individual works and of art quilts as a whole. By the end we each felt we had made a contribution, had learned from each other's perspectives, and were enriched by being exposed to such a wealth of exciting and excellent new works.

Quilts, by their constructive form, are textile sandwiches imbued by the artist with color, emotion, ideas, and stories. The use of burning, transparency, color removal, paint addition, surface design embellishments of all kinds, simple and elaborate stitchery, as well as the use of words and poetry present the viewer with the totality and essence of a quilt. Ideally, each element of design and technique is chosen to create a specific language in support of the artist's concept. Finally, it is the dialogue presented, the interaction with the viewer, that distinguishes a quilt and commands our interest and time.

There was a high number of superb quilts among the 1,232 entries for this year's Quilt National, making final selections extremely difficult. Given the chance, we would have happily chosen twice the number of quilts for exhibition. Over three days we viewed each quilt at least three times, and most were seen four times. We tried to eliminate quilts that were simply derivative of more established artists' works and focused instead on pieces that had a fresh approach, originality, and a clear voice.

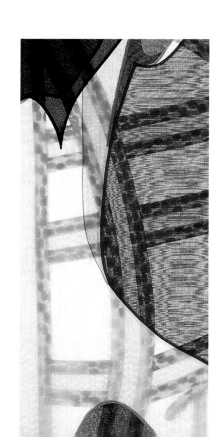

We found multiple uses of ideas among the entries, varying levels of intellectual interest, and confidence in the use of materials. There were fewer pieced quilts; artists tended to rely more on creating their own fabric. Most pieces had a real definition to them, even if they were not successful.

In deliberating about our selections, one question was often raised: why is this a quilt and not a painting or a tapestry? An excellent example of a quilt that satisfies this question is Petra Soesemann's *Men, Women: Chapter 1,* which won Best of Show. This piece pushes the boundaries of the quilt form to produce subtle and mysteriously transparent images that are uniquely suited to her idea. Her references to movement, solid mass, evolution, travel, and basic humanity are pulled together in a way that is possible only with a double-sided quilt format.

Another award-winning quilt, Karen Perrine's *Remains of the Day,* illustrates the way in which quilts can produce textural depth with a balance of innovative techniques, giving the viewer a lasting imprint of the artist's personal involvement.

Many pieces in the show deserved recognition, and we decided to give three jurors' awards in addition to the awards typically given by Quilt National. Once we had made our final selections, we were excited that in this year's Quilt National there are several works by more established artists taking

13

Left: Detail. Petra Soesemann. See pages 16 & 17.

Above: Detail. Therese May. See pages 96 & 97.

Right: Detail. Jane Burch Cochran. See page 55.

risks and moving in new directions as well as a number of first-time exhibitors. While we believe this is a very strong show, the quilts selected were not the only "good" quilts submitted for consideration. (One morning all three of us came to breakfast with concerns about the previous day's decisions after having dreamt about quilts all night.) By Sunday we felt confident that the works we chose had intriguing visual impact and contributed to a diverse and cohesive exhibition.

The jurying process was made enjoyable and manageable thanks to the dedicated and efficient staff at the Dairy Barn. In particular, we are grateful to Susan Urano, executive director of the Dairy Barn Cultural Arts Center, and Hilary Fletcher, Quilt National project director, whose boundless energy and enthusiasm for the art quilt are matched only by her professionalism. The Dairy Barn should be commended for its leadership role in promoting the art quilt and touring Quilt National exhibitions throughout the country. Finally, we thank all of the artists who entered this year's competition and who have worked to advance this very exciting art field.

Our hope is that the works in this year's Quilt National exhibition will challenge the viewer to thoroughly study the ideas presented, to notice the materials and methods of construction, and to discover in what way each quilt is unique yet part of a centuries-old tradition of self-expression in the quilt form. We also hope you will come away from this experience, as we did, feeling enriched and invigorated about the work being done today in contemporary art quilts.

-Ann Batchelder
-Libby Lehman
-Linda MacDonald

15

It's up there on the wall, sliced in half like a horizon between the sky and the ground, between reality and myth, or between preconceived attitudes and the truth. It is my hope that you are drawn in by the light and not fooled by the writing.

Jeanne Lyons Butler
Huntington, New York

The Writing's on The Wall

Commercial and hand-dyed cotton, silk, and synthetic fabrics; machine pieced and quilted; 56 x 60 inches.

16

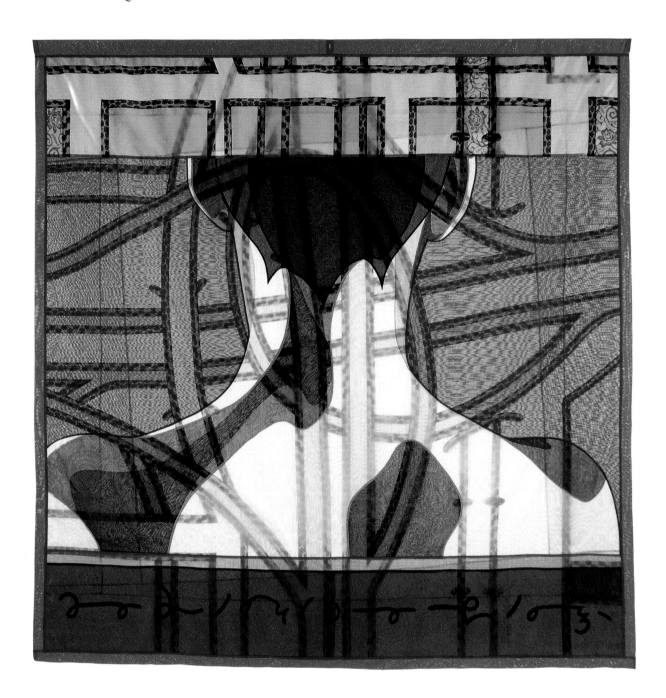

Petra Soesemann
Wooster, Ohio

**M
WOMEN, Chapter 1
N**

Natural and synthetic
fabrics; direct hand and
machine appliqué by
fusing, hand quilted;
75 x 76 inches.

Each side of this quilt is always seen through the veil of the image on the other side. The veiling effect is relative and can reveal or conceal, depending on the light. An expressway image from a Chicago map runs through a back-view self portrait to suggest an interior mapping of place, time, and female identity. The shorthand encryption reads: "Women veil their egos the way men mask their emotions."

17

**M
WOMEN, Chapter 1
N**

Reverse view.

18

Melissa Hozinger
Arlington, Washington

Circular Thinking
Canvas that has been
painted, drawn, and air-
brushed with acrylic,
pastels, and ink; layered,
fused, and machine
quilted, mounted, and
framed. 32 x 40 inches.

*My current work is about reconciling my love of the quilting
tradition with the spontaneity and pure joy of drawing and
painting. The circle has been a recurring theme in my quilts
for as long as I've been making them. Now and then I return
to an old friend with new information and new experience.*

In the "Peculiar Poetry" series, the garden, seen in different lights and weather, is the guiding inspiration. My aim is to create a sense of structure while juxtaposing strong and sometimes chaotic colors and patterns. Likewise, the inherent order of each plant form is retained as it is combined with others in a seemingly random fashion by nature, or by a gardener with more enthusiasm than forethought.

Dominie Nash
Bethesda, Maryland

Peculiar Poetry 4

Cotton and silk fabrics treated with fiber reactive dyes, screen printing with textile paint and fabric crayon; machine appliquéd and machine quilted; 43 x 43 inches.

20

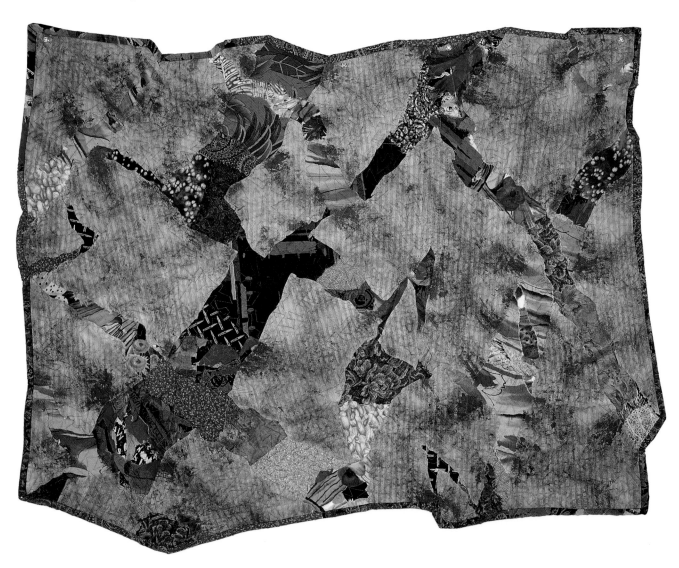

Stephanie Randall Cooper
Everett, Washington

Curse

Cotton, rayon, polyester,
silk, and blended fabrics
hand embellished with
acrylic paint; cut-and-paste
construction, machine
quilted; 58 x 47 inches.

*Each piece in this series — "Celebration of the Female/The
Uterus Series" — is intended to expose/discuss aspects of life
for women today: physiology, emotion, culture, and transformation. The irregular shape and style indicate the weaving
of a continuing story. Originating from my confusion, this
work is largely autobiographical. In a larger sense, the story
I tell could and does represent many other women with
similar tales. The story unfolds once a month.*

*I have been enamored with surfaces in most of my work —
color overlaying color, peeling surfaces, edges that define
and contrast. Now the final marks are getting larger,
more dramatic in, perhaps, a gesture to come closer
and take in all the quiet detail.*

Joan Schulze
Sunnyvale, California

The Angel Equation

Silk and cotton fabrics, paper; appliquéd, laminated, painted, pieced, and printed; machine quilted; 57 x 56 inches.

22

23

From 1917 to 1925 Frank Lloyd Wright designed a group of "Textile Block" houses built from concrete blocks cast with low-relief patterns. This inspiration came from watching Chinese weavers make rugs Wright designed for the Imperial Hotel in Tokyo. My "Emotions & Abstractions" series began with the block Wright designed and had custom-fabricated for the Millard House in Pasadena, California (1923). After slightly modifying the block and altering the "set" of blocks, I had a pattern I could work with. I then immersed myself in the subtle patterning and colors of my hand-dyed fabrics.

Liz Axford
Houston, Texas

Emotions & Abstractions 2

Cotton fabrics hand dyed by Fabrics to Dye For (Liz Axford and Connie Scheele); machine pieced and machine quilted; 80 x 45 inches.

24

Karen K. Stone
Dallas, Texas

Indian Orange Peel
Cotton fabrics, mostly
homespun, batiks, and
reproduction fabrics;
machine pieced onto
original paper foundations
and machine quilted
with rayon thread;
63 x 63 inches.

*While the fabric choices in the quilt may seem to reflect the
tension and complexity of my urban life, its inspiration is
actually the traditional orange peel quilt and an orange Indian
wedding ring quilt from the Pilgrim/Roy collection. While I've
come to associate this piece with fire and gospel music (which,
like quiltmaking, have changed little in 100 years), I think its
appeal lies in the simple juxtaposition of two opposing colors.*

Every body of water I've seen in recent years has unmistakable signs of human presence — trivial garbage like candy wrappers or foam cups. In Remains of The Day, *the time is dusk, and it's a little spooky. There is no evidence of plants or water animals. I don't know if the water is pure or polluted…it is very clear but dark. The people have gone home, leaving, as always, something behind.*

Karen Perrine
Tacoma, Washington

Remains of the Day

Cotton, sateen, and nylon tulle treated with Procion dye, fabric pigments and felt marker, cotton and metallic threads; hand painted and airbrushed, hand appliquéd, hand and machine quilted; 44 x 43 inches. From a private collection.

26

Anne Smith
Chesire, England

Catherine Wheel

Cotton blends and recycled
fabrics; machine pieced
and appliquéd, hand quilted; 52 x 53 inches.

*My previous work had been subdued in tone reflecting
a spiritual theme, and I wanted to make something in a
lighter mood. I took my inspiration from the annual Hull
Fair, the biggest in England. Starting with a small pastel
study, I arrived at the final destination by pinning and
rearranging the fabrics on a large board.*

Recently I have been painting, dyeing, spraying, and using wax resist to create my own designs on fabric. The actual application of the wax and the physicality of dyeing are interesting and enjoyable. The balance between the aspects that I can control and the elements of surprise that are always present in these processes is intriguing to me.

Nancy Taylor
Pleasanton, California

Nine Patch

Cotton fabric that has been dyed, painted, and patterned with wax resist; machine pieced and machine quilted; 47 x 51 inches.

28

Sigi Gertschen Probst
Bern, Switzerland

Ohne Titel

Mixed fiber batting,
cotton, and acrylic paint;
sewn, quilted, and
embroidered by machine,
painted; 35 x 50 inches.

*This is a whole-cloth quilt. It's a naked quilt. It's even a
skinless quilt. It is what remains if you take away the
surface of a quilt and come to the inside, where the dreams
and the lifemarks are. It's a possible content, a possible
meaning of a quilt.*

*While we think of nights as seamless, sleep-filled darkness,
they are often fragile times, easily fractured
from within and from without.*

Barbara J. Mortenson
Glenside, Pennsylvania

Fractured Nights

Collagraphs on black
organza, layered and cut
through; machine embroi-
dered with rayon and
other threads; additional
layers of hand-painted
fabrics; 22 x 27 inches.

30

Melody Johnson
Cary, Illinois

Reaching for the Light

Hand-dyed cotton fabrics,
fusible web, metallic
thread; machine
appliquéd, machine quilt-
ed; 57 x 53 inches.

*The spirit of the time is reflected in the art of the time.
Serious artists are stimulated to produce work that deals
with despair, conflict, and chaos, and the breakdown of contemporary society. If one lives with a spirit of optimism, one
risks being considered a Pollyanna. Nevertheless, for me,
making optimistic art is my remedy for a discouraged world.
Instead of reflecting negativity, I hope to reveal a way out of
the darkness, a way to reach for the light.*

31

ROOKIE AWARD

I have been working on a series of quilts using windows as a theme — both in the literal and in the metaphorical sense. The literal choice of the window motif is probably because I come from a northern country, needing light, and seeing ruined abbeys with open sky windows. Metaphorically, windows reflect my interest in self-growth and understanding.

Elizabeth Barton
Athens, Georgia

**Windows XIII:
Aiming High**

Hand-dyed and commercial cotton fabrics; machine pieced and appliquéd, machine quilted with rayon and metallic thread; 41 x 67 inches.

Colorado's Anasazi cliff dwellings challenged me to depict the stonework's visual texture along with the subtle colorations and shadows of the light-colored sandstone. My hand-dyed fabrics create nuances of jewel-like areas glimpsed through an otherwise determined color field, with these "color jewels" suggesting mystique and depth. My interpretation is inspired by Monet's brush strokes and his depiction of nature's light and color by using awesome tints and hues.

Patty Hawkins
Lyons, Colorado

Anasazi Dwellings: Colors Stratified

Cotton fabrics, some hand dyed by the artist, painted and chalk-marked canvas; random strip-piecing and direct machine appliquéd, machine quilted; 69 x 38 inches.

34

Sara Long
Fort Bragg, California
AIDS Web
Cotton fabric, canceled
AIDS stamps made into
buttons, hand pieced and
hand quilted; 46 x 34 inches.

AIDS Web *is a historical piece regarding the political
and social implications of AIDS. This is an important piece
to me because AIDS has directly affected my own life.*

My interest in space and landscape comes from growing up on the continent's western edge. At night we could see ten thousand stars curving to the far horizon. My dreams thrust me into those spaces: cold, distant, yet somehow familiar. When the astronauts landed and took their first lunar steps, I was giving birth to our son. In the cold light of the delivery room, I saw the stars in his eyes.

Judith Tomlinson Trager
Boulder, Colorado

Lunarscape

Cotton, rayon, and silk fabrics; machine pieced in crazy quilt technique, machine quilted and hand painted; 57 x 61 inches.

36

Suzanne Evenson
Worthington, Ohio

Birds in the House I

Cotton and translucent
synthetic fabrics that have
been embellished with
beads, cloth fragments,
and hand stitching;
machine pieced, quilted,
and appliquéd; 42 x
45 inches.

*The inspiration for this quilt is an old wives' tale told to me
by my mother: a bird in the house tells of a warning. As a
child, just before a fire at her farm, a bird was in her house.
Years later, as I struggled with a difficult situation, a bird
pecking daily on the window of my studio was a warning
that my center — my creative soul — was in danger.
Birds are protective spiritual entities.*

I am working on a series of quilts that explore traditional female roles and domestic objects in a whimsical way. This quilt is my way of playfully ridiculing the classical role of women as caretakers, pretending all the while that everything is perfect. Nothing is wrong and, in fact, it is a wonderful life. If only one could see beneath the smile.

Wendy C. Huhn
Dexter, Oregon

It's a Wonderful Life

Hand-dyed and commercial cottons embellished with paint, glue transfers, and glitter; machine pieced and machine quilted; 64 x 64 inches.

38

Alex Fuhr
Oxford, Ohio

Spelling

Procion hand-dyed rayon
challis and cotton woolsey;
machine pieced and hand
quilted; 83 x 81 inches.

Spelling *refers to something elementary at which I was
always horrible but at which through sheer force of will
I made myself successful. So too my naive quilting skills
have evolved by trial and error into a composition with which
I am satisfied. I am aiming for the kind of "abstract impres-
sionism" often found in fine ethnic textiles. This quilt can
function as and is constructed as a blanket. But at the same
time it is hanging on the wall as art. The image, the material, the process, and therefore the object are interdependent.
They are the same thing. Its composition, both color and line,
and also its structure combine to create an emotional impact.*

This piece is part of a series exploring space and other formal values with as much economy as I can bring to it. By removing the seduction of texture and excessive piecing, I tried to keep my focus on the formal concerns of the piece.

Linda Levin
Wayland, Massachusetts

Composition IV

Procion dyed cotton fabrics, flannel batting; machine appliquéd and machine quilted; 30 x 40 inches.

40

Jane Dunnewold
San Antonio, Texas

Baby Quilt
Solvent transfers on silk
habotai with mattress pad,
gold foil on blanket binding,
burned birthday candles;
machine quilted and em-
broidered; 36 x 42 inches.

*I struggle regularly with the challenge of mothering. My
daughter Zenna has, without even trying, taught me more
about grace, truth, and laughter than I ever set out to learn.
This quilt expresses that bittersweet love combined with the
"letting go" that all parents face if they are doing it right.
The words are borrowed from Kalil Gibran's* The Prophet.

MOST INNOVATIVE USE OF THE MEDIUM AWARD
Sponsored by Friends of Fiber Art International

The indomitability of the human spirit may be the most magnificent gift God has given us. Despite hardships endured by body and soul, we all have the capacity to rise above difficult circumstances to become more powerful in spirit.

Ann Curtis
Burke, Virginia

Epicenter of My Soul

Commercial and hand-dyed fabrics by Debra Lunn and Michael Mrowka, commercial and hand-dyed perle cotton by Melody Johnson, Facile®; multilayered, open-centered faced modules set into faced openings in whole-cloth background; hand quilted; 53 x 53 inches.

JURORS' AWARD OF MERIT

Breathing can be seen as a metaphor for communication. When one takes a breath, that breath is an exchange, inhale/exhale, a give and take. To be healthy, cooperation among all parts must exist. In Breathe color is used to suggest both the structure and movement of a breath. Within the light areas to the left and right of the green center, brush strokes resemble the turbulence of air movement. This becomes further activated by the mostly horizontal thin fabric lines and quilted lines that carry parameter and center colors back and forth across the quilt's expanse.

Erika Carter
Bellevue, Washington

Breathe

Hand-painted cotton and silk organza fabrics; machine appliquéd and machine quilted; 71 x 46 inches.

44

Elizabeth A. Busch
Bangor, Maine

Float

Textile inks and acrylics
on canvas; painted,
airbrushed, and hand
quilted; 40 x 28 inches.

*Contrasts in temperature, materials and methods, and ideas
and attitudes are the focus of my painted quilts. I create
special ambiguities that put the viewer in different places at
the same time — inside and outside, awake and dreaming.
I draw upon my own everyday experiences for imagery.
The last steps in the process, hand quilting and embroidery,
allow me to become physically reacquainted with a piece
created at arm's length on the wall, and to add another
visual dimension to it.*

My interest in old stuff and structures has found inspiration outside and a few steps from our rural central Florida home. It's called my husband's work shed. In my new series of quilts I use black and white photography to capture and manipulate these images. I transfer the images onto cloth using the silkscreen process.

Fran Skiles
Plantation, Florida

Thread Bare I

Cotton duck, silk and nylon toile, fabric paint, ink, silk paint, resist, photo transfers, and yarn embellishments; silk screened, machine pieced, and machine quilted; 60 x 55 inches.

46

Nancy Crow
Baltimore, Ohio
Color Blocks #41
Pima cottons all hand
dyed by Nancy Crow;
machine pieced by the
artist, hand quilted by
Marla Hattabaugh;
51 x 41 inches.

Color Blocks #41 *resulted from my own improvisational process called "floaters." I cut shapes into a background fabric directly as though I am drawing with a pencil. As it is very difficult to make corrections, I try to be very focused so that <u>each cut is beautiful the first time</u>. The process takes hours of practice. The process and I become one as all the cuts are extensions of how I see and how I feel about the shapes that develop spontaneously. This is the most challenging way I have ever worked because it is <u>so direct</u> with no intellectual preparation done beforehand and no templates made.*

By hand printing and painting each unit, my intent was to create a whole-cloth wall quilt with an image or pattern that related to traditional piecing. The process allows me to connect and build the pieces and produce a compound fabric surface with paint, color, and hand quilting.

Lenore Davis
Newport, Kentucky

Montana Aspens

Cotton velveteen, poly batting, textile paint, dye, and cotton thread; monotype, and painting; hand quilted with tailor's serging stitch; 60 x 60 inches.

48

Alison F. Whittemore
San Antonio, Texas

**Just One Cup
Before I Go**

Fabric treated with
Procion dyes, ink draw-
ings, phototransfers, iron-
on stars, and beads;
machine appliquéd and
machine quilted; 39 x
51 inches.

*This quilt is one of a series called "Quiltmaker in Hell."
I began it as a healing process after my divorce and subse-
quent major life upheavals. The woman, a symbol of myself,
stands stripped and stunned amid symbols of death and the
afterlife that indicate the end of one major phase of her life.*

49

Most of my quilts are abstract representations of my personal response to the landscape and sky of my native New Mexico. They are personal landscapes reflecting my deeply held belief that "God's eternal power and deity are clearly perceived in the things that He has created." I painted the center portion of this quilt after the Phillipine volcano Pinatubo erupted. The resulting ash in the upper atmosphere created sunsets in New Mexico that were even more spectacular than usual.

Katy J. Widger
Edgewood, New Mexico

Pinatubo: Fire in The Sky

Hand-dyed and painted cottons; machine pieced and machine quilted with cotton and rayon threads; 51 x 50 inches.

*My studio was packed in boxes, my life was on hold,
and I was waiting for my contractor. After 18 years of
deferred maintenance, we were renovating the house.
I moved out for three months with a dozen fabrics, some
thread, and a sewing machine. The results of those
limitations are* Good and Plenty *and the recognition
that fewer choices often prove liberating.*

Judy Becker
Newton, Massachusetts

**Good and Plenty:
While Waiting for
My Contractor**

Cotton, cotton chintz,
batik, and drapery fabric;
machine pieced and
machine quilted; 82 x
48 inches (combined mea-
surement of both pieces).

52

Meredyth L. Colberg
Fox River Grove, Illinois
Snakes and Ladders
Cotton fabrics airbrushed
with Procion fiber reactive
dyes; machine pieced and
machine quilted;
47 x 34 inches.

The journey from fabric to finish is a constant inner dialogue of questioning, experimentation, stepping back, observing, and listening to one's instincts. There are clues to follow along the way for the patient observer who has the ability to play. An exciting surface design could be a springboard. A quick thumbnail sketch might ground the energy. The creative toolbox, tapped for the skills to verify the vision. The journey, the creative process itself, is what I love most.

53

I consider Organica *as representing the interconnectedness of all life — the Universal Oneness. I didn't set out to make this particular statement. It just evolved and took its own direction as if the quilt were already out there in the ether and it was my task to help it materialize. Airbrushes constantly clog and splatter, requiring constant problem solving. You have to develop a sort of "happy masochism" in order to stay with this technique, I think.*

Peg Bird
Yellow Springs, Ohio

Organica

Cotton fabrics treated with airbrush and pen; machine quilted; 34 x 47 inches.

54

Leslie Gabriëlse
Rotterdam, The Netherlands
Enlarged Apple
Fabric and acrylic paint;
hand appliquéd, quilted,
and painted; 85 x 53 inches.

Enlarged Apple *was influenced by a work by French Impressionist painter Pierre Bonnard. That work was almost entirely orange except for some small additions of other colors. The yellow fabric used in this piece was recycled from one of the environmental sculptures by Christo, a well-known contemporary artist.*

In rural Kentucky, you still see a few clotheslines. I love to see the clothes waving in the breeze. They tell a story about a family. Life Line *is a self-portrait: part gypsy butterfly, part pearly queen, part moon chaser. The pearly kings and queens are a group of Cockney English who cover their clothes with buttons and collect alms for the poor. The turkey buzzard is a bird I see every day. It looks so beautiful when it is flying and soaring, but up close it is ugly by our standards. Perhaps made of beads and silks, it seems more beautiful.*

Jane Burch Cochran
Rabbit Hash, Kentucky

Life Line
Various fabrics and old clothing that have been treated with paint and colored pencils, beads, and buttons; hand appliquéd, hand beaded and embellished; 82 x 68 inches.

56

Nancy N. Erickson
Missoula, Montana

**The Models Have
Been Waiting for
Some Time, But No
Artist Is in Sight**

Cotton, satin, and velvet
fabrics embellished with
fabric paint; machine
stitched and appliquéd;
60 x 60 inches.

This work, the ninth in a series about studio life, illustrates the true situation in my own work room, where my companions (and I) are sometimes late, or not ready, when the model is. I move back and forth from painting with paintsticks to working on a larger scale with quilting and fabrics. Each approach enhances the other.

57

Early in 1994, I returned to my island home from Houston with a suitcase filled with hand-dyed fabrics and an idea for a new quilt. As I worked on the quilt, the name Local Color came to me. Living on an island buffered from the mainland by Puget Sound, I find the importance of local people is magnified. The variety of colors in the quilt reflects the diverse, vibrant personalities of the island population.

Janet Steadman
Clinton, Washington

Local Color

Cotton fabrics, most of which were hand dyed by Liz Axford and Connie Scheele; machine pieced and hand quilted; 58 x 58 inches.

58

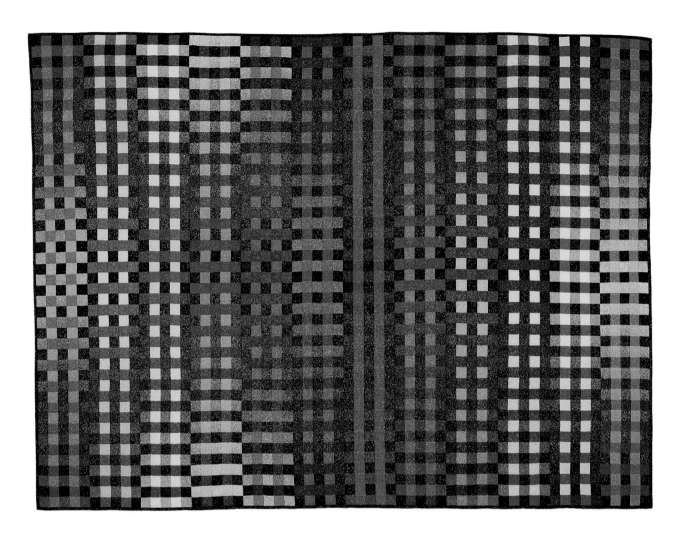

Michael Mrowka
Denver, Colorado

**Michael's Excellent
Color Adventure**

Pointillist Palette (a signa-
ture line of fabric designed
by Michael Mrowka and
Debra Lunn for Robert
Kaufman Co. Inc);
machine pieced and quilt-
ed with assistance by
Elaine Cottingham;
87 x 64 inches.

*Using principles of color theory, with gradual gradations of
color moving from selvage to selvage, Pointillist Palette puts
"paint in a tube" for quiltmakers. The 264 different colors
used in this quilt were cut from only 24 colorways. Taking
advantage of the gradations and using strip piecing techniques,
this quilt — my third — was truly a color adventure.*

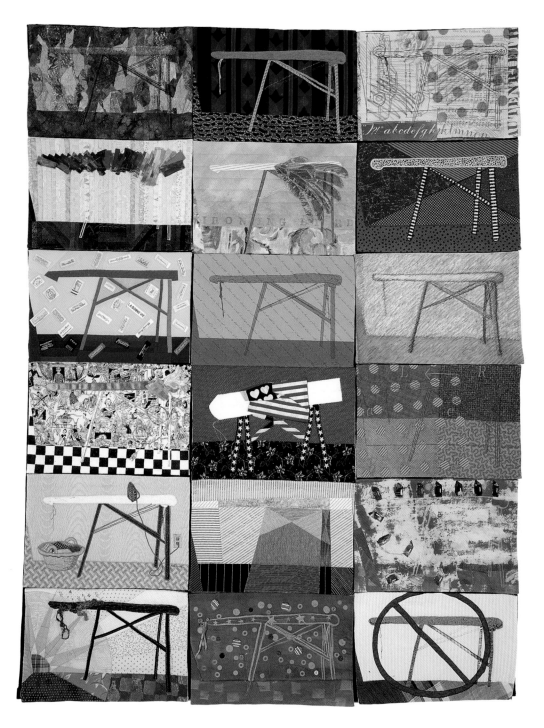

59

Never Done *is the fifth in a series of collaborative works by New Image members. We worked from a photograph taken by Dominie Nash who initiated this piece. Keeping the shape, size, and placement the same, each artist approached the ironing board image with her own style, technique, and emotions. Ironing boards symbolically stand astride the line between our personal and artistic lives for those of us working with fabric.*
New Image members include: Pat Autenreith, Barbara Bockman, Carol Gersen, Lesly-Claire Greenberg, Dorothy Holden, Dominie Nash, Sue Pierce, Mary Ann Rush, Judy Spahn, Linda Tilton, Michele Vernon, and Caroline Wooden.

New Image*
Virginia and Maryland

Never Done

Various fabrics and materials embellished with rubber stamps, fabric crayons, embroidery, Inkoprinting, and cyanotype; hand and machine pieced, appliquéd, and quilted; 54 x 72 inches.

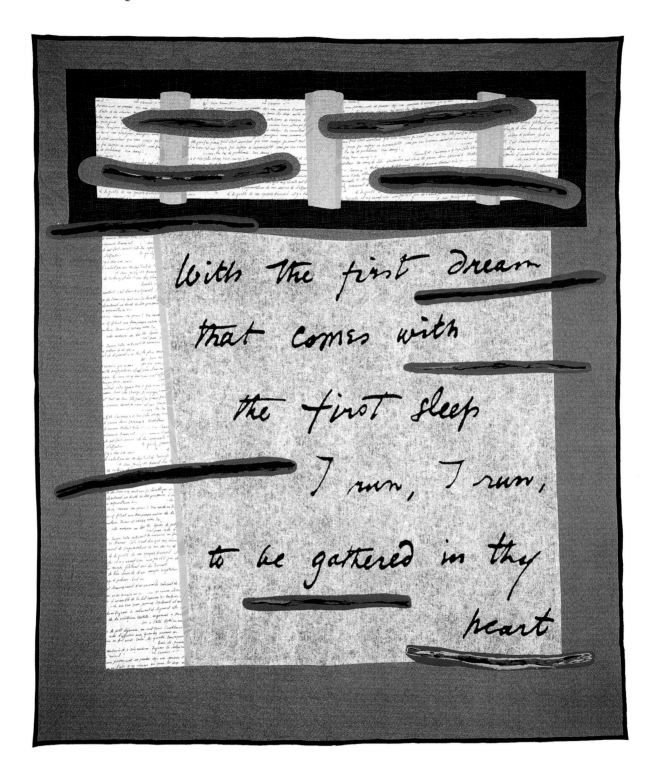

With the first dream
that comes with
the first sleep
I run, I run,
to be gathered in thy
heart

60

Robin Schwalb
Brooklyn, New York

First Dream

Commercial and stenciled
cottons and cotton/linen
blends; machine pieced,
hand appliquéd, and hand
quilted; 77 x 89 inches.

*I liked the idea of making a quilt about sleeping and dreaming.
I also wanted the chosen text, after a poem by Alice Meynell, to
be a major design element. Begun in May 1992 while visiting
Susi Shie and Jimmy Acord (a.k.a. "Zombie Quilt Camp"),*
First Dream *was an exercise in working with only the
limited palette of fabrics I had brought from home.*

Interior #5 is from a series of quilts and paintings based on doors and chairs. I was interested in discovering a connection between oil painting on canvas and painting with dyes on fabric. Initially I bought a pair of French doors and an old chair that I drew, photographed, photocopied, and collaged. The resulting quilts are based on the fractured black and white collage. Metaphorically, they refer to not only a physical interior, but also to the interiors of the mind.

Clare M. Murray
Canton, Ohio

Interior #5

Various fabrics including nylon net, cheesecloth, and sheers, painted with fiber reactive dyes; machine appliquéd and machine quilted; 90 x 68 inches.

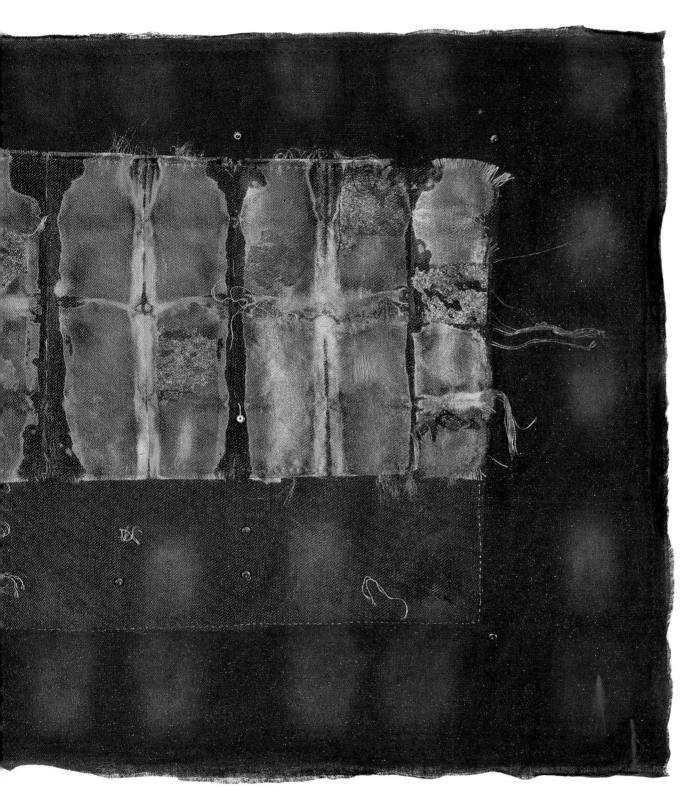

In my work I have been exploring the use of visual grid structures. Relic Vessels *refers to the forms suggested in the discharged fabric; fragments of ritual, relics obscured by layers of time.*

Patricia Mink
Ann Arbor, Michigan

Relic Vessels

Hand-dyed cotton, discharged acetate, netting, gold leaf, fabric paint, and beads; appliquéd; 38 x 20 inches.

64

Nancy Condon
Stillwater, Minnesota

Idols of Reality

Cotton and linen fabrics embellished with chalk, fabric paint, and embroidery threads; mostly hand sewn with some machine construction and hand tied; 90 x 70 inches.

This quilt was made by drawing directly on the material with chalk and tearing away part of the double fabric to expose a figure beneath. The construction was minimal with simple tying leaving exposed edges and frayed fabric.

This approach was intended to be direct, to explore the qualities of the materials, and mostly to enhance the strength of the images. Even reality is raw and direct sometimes.

*In 1993 I received a grant from the Empire State Crafts
Alliance to explore nontoxic intaglio printing on cloth.
I bought an etching press and began making collagraphs
using environmentally safe printing methods. I was more
concerned with materials and process than content and
subject matter. But as the prints emerged, I realized that
I had unconsciously incorporated images that reflected
my concern for the environment and my own health
as an artist, the motivating idea behind the project.*

Karen Felicity Berkenfeld
New York, New York

Where There's Smoke

Cotton printed with
collagraph printing plates
on an etching press using
Grumbacher MAX water-
soluble, oil-based paint;
machine pieced and hand
quilted; 36 x 46 inches.

66

Susan Webb Lee
Weddington, North Carolina

Red Threads

Hand-dyed cotton fabrics;
machine pieced and
machine quilted;
39 x 51 inches.

Dyed fabrics are placed in small compartments of varying sizes and shapes. The red edging emphasizes certain areas or lines, and the erratic quilting pattern flows from one "block" to another, connecting and integrating the shapes. The circular motifs represent continuity and security while the squares refer to diversity, exploration, and the search for an adventurous spirit.

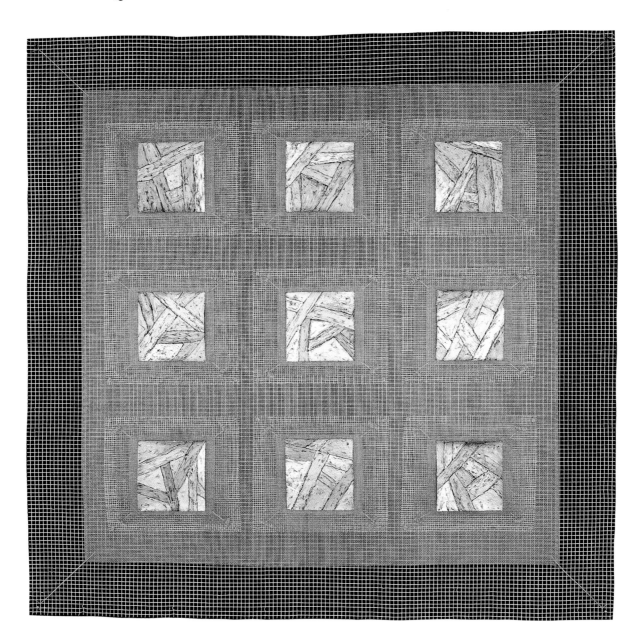

Art parallels progress, modern industry, and invention. These influences create new forms of expression and aesthetics. My "Industrial Quilts" embody the aesthetic quality and confusion of machine-made versus hand-made. I use unconventional materials that complement each other yet provoke the controversy surrounding the way things of value are made. Contrasts such as delicate versus durable, structure versus freedom, decorative versus conceptual, intimate versus impersonal aim at a new aesthetic influenced by tradition and progress.

Anne Marie Kenny
Hooksett, New Hampshire

Woven II Industrial Quilt

Acrylic paint on cotton canvas, steel and bronze wire cloth, fiberglass mesh, spray paint, wire, and thread; paintings stitched by hand with wire and thread; 37 x 36 inches.

68

*Conscious and unconscious absorption of color and pattern
drive my quiltmaking. When the April 1994 issue of* National
Geographic *arrived on my doorstep just after I finished a
quilt of the New Zealand bush colors, the completely different
desert colors shown with the article on John Wesley Powell said
to me, "Another quilt." Representation of the juxtaposition of
colors in nature through a "double colorwash" of lattice and
picture has evolved from a variety of experiments.*

Marge Hurst
Pukerua Bay, Wellington,
New Zealand

**Tribute to John
Wesley Powell**

Commercial and hand-
dyed cotton and blended
fabrics; machine pieced
and machine quilted;
78 x 49 inches.

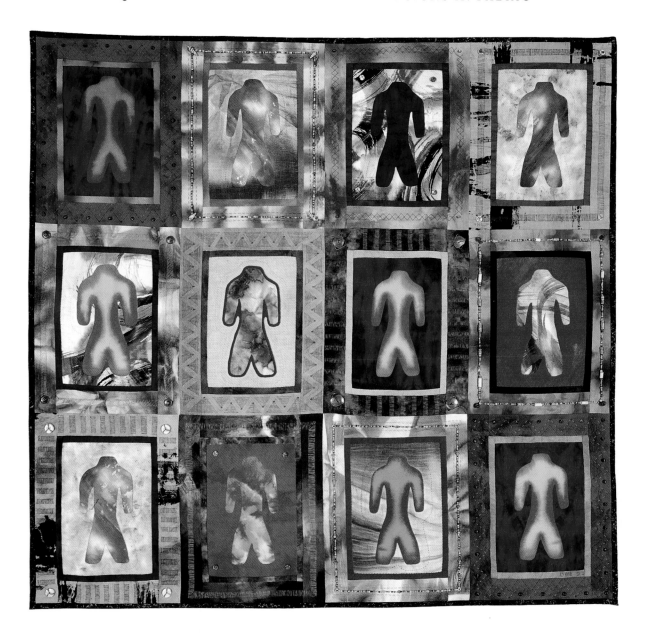

70

Diana Whitmer-
Francko
Oxford, Ohio

**Trade Routes (Ancient
Culture Series)**

Commercial and hand-
dyed cotton fabrics
embellished with beads,
shells and handmade cop-
per buttons; reverse
appliquéd, machine
pieced, and hand quilted;
38 x 36 inches.

*I have been fascinated and intrigued by the images associat-
ed with ancient cultures, especially the Hopewell and Adena
cultures in Ohio. This particular quilt is the third in the
series on "Ancient Cultures." It is my visual concept of the
trade routes through which ancient tribes were able to pro-
cure materials not native to their own environments.*

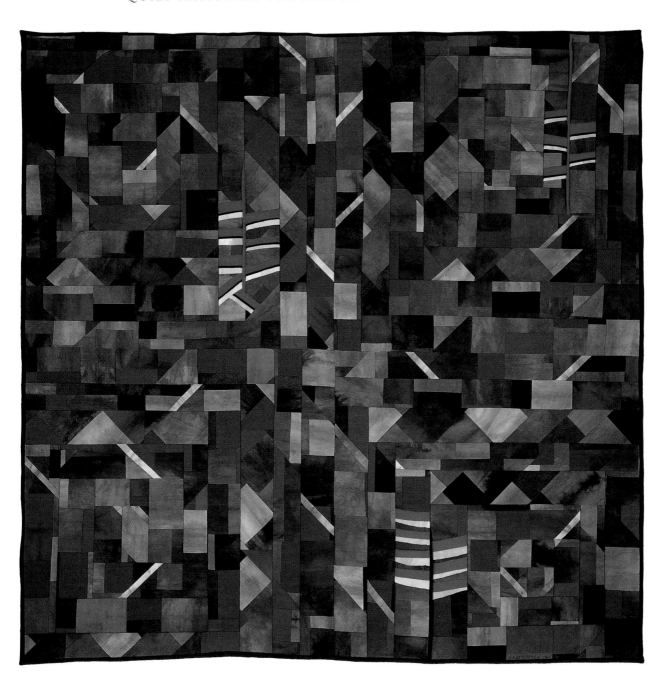

Making a quilt frees me up intuitively to develop an idea.
The inspiration for this piece arose from a recent trip
to the rain forests of Costa Rica. Thank you, Walter.

Edith C. Mitchell
Tupper Lake, New York

**Intuit Square IV:
Heliconia**

Hand-dyed cottons by
Lunn Fabrics and Fabrics
to Dye For, cotton batting;
machine strip-pieced and
repieced, machine stitched
and quilted in one opera-
tion; 44 x 44 inches.

72

Patricia
Kennedy-Zafred
Pittsburgh, Pennsylvania

Innocenza Persa

Commercial fabrics and
fabrics hand dyed by Jan
Myers-Newbury, Kodalith
negatives and positives
transferred to acetate;
machine pieced and
machine quilted;
16 x 20 inches.

*This piece reflects on issues of betrayal, entanglement, and
lost innocence. My recent work involves personal experiences
that are universal human emotions. Each piece is interpreted
within the context of the viewer's own experiences, thus
allowing a multitude of impressions and conclusions.
There is no right or wrong answer. I seek to provoke
thought and create impact, even if momentary.*

Crazy Rose resulted from two classic housekeeping problems: an inability to throw anything away and a lack of storage space. For years, my garment business, Kaleidoscope Clothing, has generated boxes of my hand-dyed and printed fabric scraps. Rose grew from those boxes. She didn't deplete the boxes by a long shot but she did grow to be my inspiration for more quilts. Her sisters may emerge during spring cleaning.

Laura Wasilowski
Elgin, Illinois

Crazy Rose
Cotton fabrics that have been hand dyed, painted, stamped, and silk screened; machine pieced and machine quilted; 41 x 35 inches.

74

David Walker
Cincinnati, Ohio

Passing Through

Netting and cotton fabrics,
some of which have been
bleached and overdyed;
machine appliquéd,
machine quilted, and
machine embroidered,
hand stamped and embell-
ished with beads;
48 x 41 inches.

This quilt is dedicated to my friend Charlie Bolan who died on May 30, 1995 from complications of the AIDS virus. Exactly one year later, Passing Through, *the first in a series of three quilts, began as a simple statement of how I had tired of grieving. I decided to throw all my unexpressed grief out into the universe, a fitting container, large enough for the stars and the planets and surely large enough to care for my grief as well. I believe that a new constellation now brightens the night sky. I know that Charlie would have it no other way.*

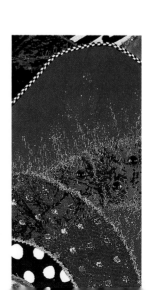

The title was chosen upon finishing the piece and is used to suggest the connection between the number of grains of sand on a beach, the number of people that have walked upon this earth, and the number of stars that we can see in the sky. I want my quilts to be beautiful, but also to suggest various ideas, meanings, and metaphors to different people. Using a whole-cloth, dye-painting technique blurs the distinction between painting and quilting, and encourages people to wonder about how we define art.

Barbara Otto
Lake Elmo, Minnesota

Space: Grains of Sand
Cotton muslin stamped with thickened Procion H dyes, resist; machine quilted whole-cloth piece; 63 x 72 inches.

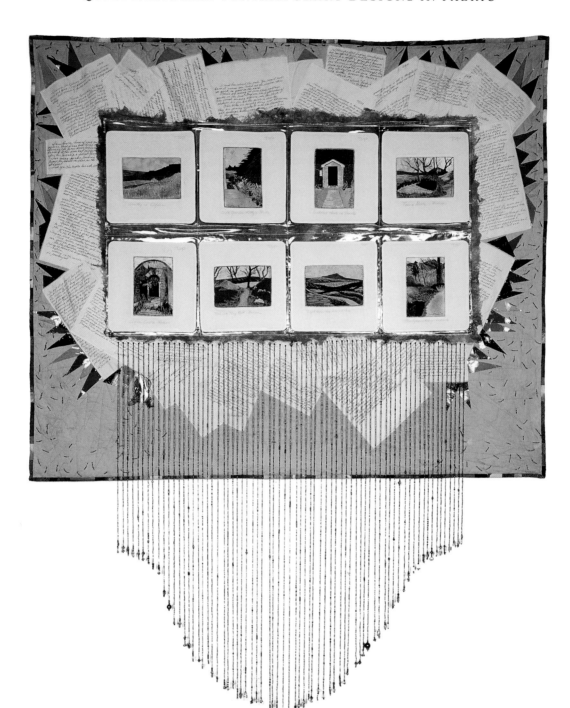

76

Donna M. Fleming
Durango, Colorado

Reredos, Prayer for Return…

Cotton fabrics dyed with commercial and vegetable dyes, metallic threads, theater gels, plastic beads and buttons; hand appliquéd, hand quilted, and a variety of other techniques necessary to achieve the desired look; 54 x 74 inches.

To bring a dream to life, one must first make an act, sort of open a door into this world through which the dream can "become." Reredos, a chronicle of a pilgrimage to ancestral lands, is that first step. That step is the first in the journey to Ireland, the fulfillment of a lifelong dream. A prayer, "reredos," opens the door for my return.

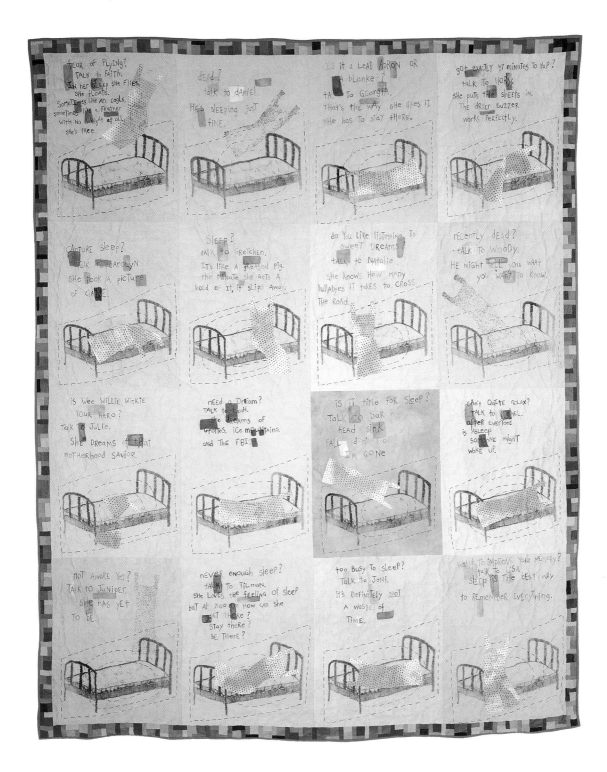

I collected these sleep epigrams from a group of friends over the course of several months. They are reflections on that most wonderful activity — sleep. In some cultures, sleep is seen as a rehearsal for death. I composed two of these epigrams in memory of two friends who recently died.

Rachel Brumer
Seattle, Washington

Conked Out

Commercial and hand-dyed cottons by Lunn Fabrics and Fabrics to Dye For, paint, fabric sensitizer; contact painted, hand appliquéd, machine pieced, and hand quilted; 61 x 75 inches.

78

INVITATIONAL WORK: QUILT NATIONAL '95 JUROR

Linda R. MacDonald
Willits, California

My Friends 2

Cotton fabric that has
been hand dyed, air-
brushed, and hand
painted; hand quilted;
40 x 36 inches.

*These shapes were familiar to me once they became visible.
They allude to the micro yet seem at home in their actual
size. This piece is part of a series of "Friends" of mine.*

79

In Sampler I: Dream House, *I am referring to the idea of home as an embodiment of idealizations which can range from nostalgia to idealized utopia. This piece is based on the "sampler" quilt format.*

Gerry Chase
Seattle, Washington

**Sampler I:
Dream House**

Cotton fabric, photo transfers, India ink, acrylic paint, and various embellishments; hand appliquéd, machine pieced, and machine quilted. 53 x 42 inches.

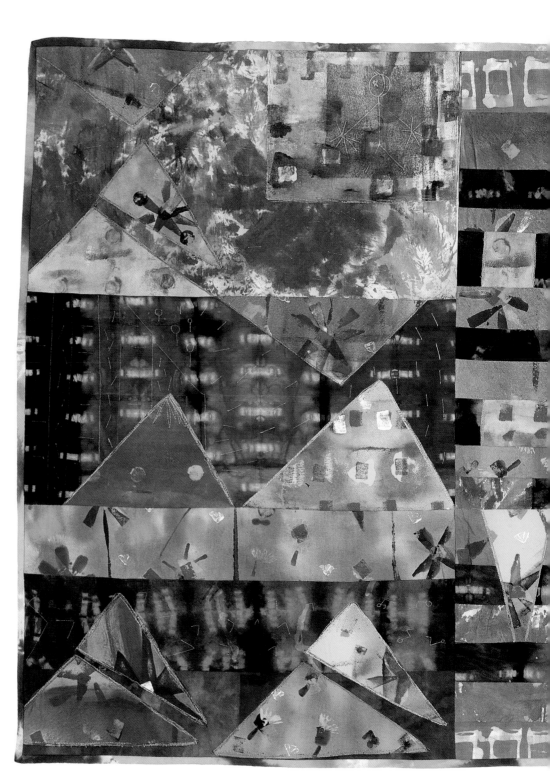

Every year I climb to a high mountain meadow as an emotional pilgrimage to reflect on my search for romantic love. Everything seems possible up there. I have experienced perfect beauty along with doubt, disbelief, and danger. I have gotten lost and scared and have been run off the mountain by a dangerous storm. In this piece I am reminding myself as I climb/search to appreciate the beauty of both the mountain flowers and the rocks below.

JoAnn Fitsell
Denver, Colorado

**The Meadow
Above Me**

Canvas and cottons treated by batik and stamping with acrylic paint and Procion dyes; machine pieced, appliquéd, and quilted; 76 x 43 inches.

82

Libby Lehman
Houston, Texas

Free Fall

Cotton, purchased hand-
dyed fabrics embellished
with machine embroidery
using rayon metallic and
Sulky Silver threads;
machine pieced and
machine quilted;
41 x 41 inches.

*I am currently exploring the design possibilities of machine
embroidery. Some embroidery was done prior to piecing and
some was added later. I like to work intuitively, letting the
quilt emerge rather than planning ahead.*

83

DON'T BUG US. | Katherine L. McKearn
and Diane Muse
Townson, Maryland and
Madrid, Iowa

Psycho-Moms at Rest
Commercial cottons and
various found items
including a pot holder,
old tablecloth, and '50s
drapery fabric; hand
appliquéd, machine
pieced, and hand quilted;
59 x 80 inches.

84

Nina Morti
Carbondale, Illinois

Sityatki Whales

Cotton fabric hand dyed
by Eric Morti, silk, Sulky
threads, batting; fabric
collage with hand and
machine stitching;
32 x 42 inches.

*When my son was three years old, he gave me a picture of
"whales" that he had drawn with markers. He had simply
sprawled on the floor and gone to work. I watched as he
worked with the pure abandon I envied. I had been reading
about petroglyphs and his "whales" reminded me of
ancient art, so I decided to use his drawing as a basis
for a representation of painting on rocks.*

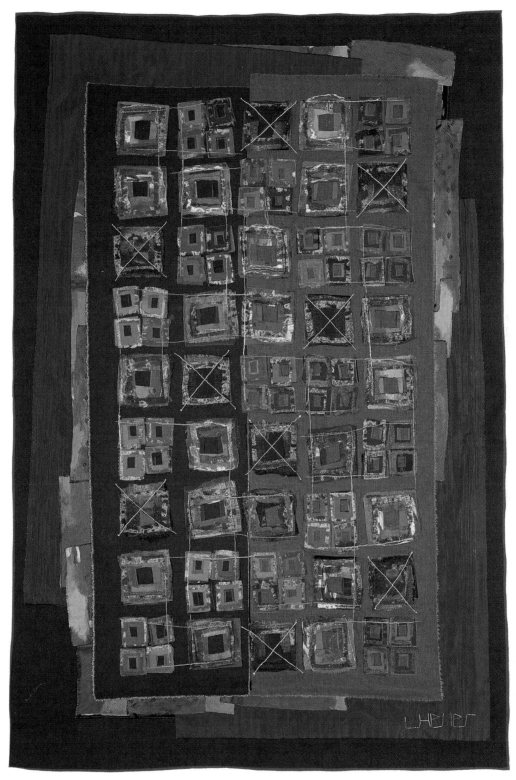

The tactile pleasure of manipulating fabric has encouraged me to explore age-old techniques of layering and stitching to create a hybrid of quiltmaking and molas (reverse appliqué) technique. I used the grid motifs and repeat patterns of quilts to establish a visual structure. Then, by cutting through the fabric, I expose the layers underneath the surface, creating depth and interest with an improvisational quality.

Lynne Heller
Toronto, Ontario, Canada

**Blue/Orange
Mola/Quilt**

Cotton, silk, silk organza, polyester organza, rayon, and wool; hand and machine stitched; 36 x 54 inches.

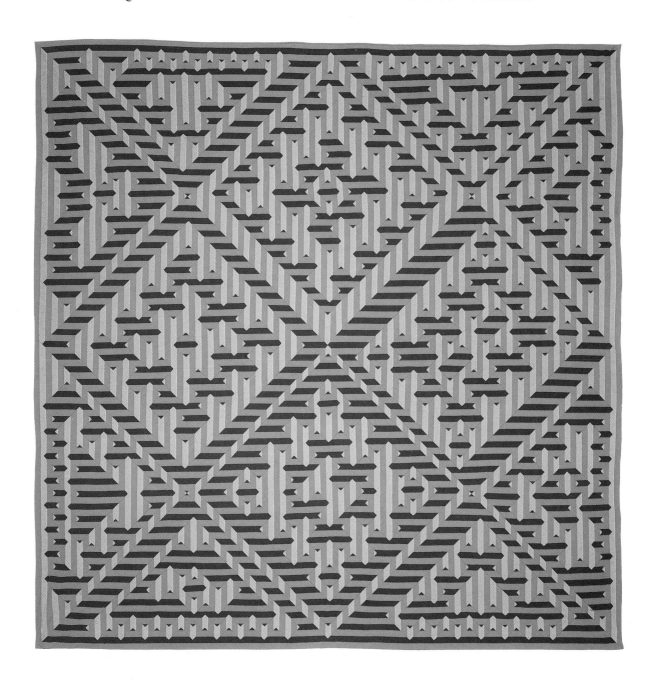

86

Ellen Oppenheimer
Oakland, California

Head Gasket Maze

Silkscreened and hand-
dyed fabric; machine sewn
and hand quilted; 60 x
60 inches.

*In 1990 I began a series of quilts that were concerned with
lines and stripes. These frequently take on the quality of a
labyrinth or maze. The series has been immensely satisfying
because I am able to address color, form, and content in a
compelling format. I feel these pieces also refer to various historical or ethnic textiles. In* Head Gasket Maze *I am particularly interested in exploring a new palette of dyes and inks.*

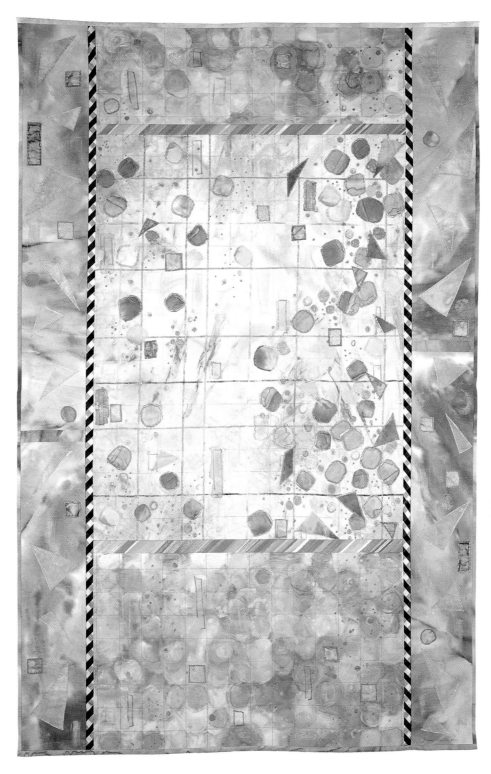

A basic grid configuration anchors the design, circular brush strokes and appliquéd shapes are confined within the geometric form of the grid. Rectangles, squares, and triangles also appear as appliquéd and painted shapes. A variety of techniques were used to paint the different fabrics. The narrow black and white vertical bands echo the subtle pastel diagonal painted horizontal bands adding an element of surprise to the composition.

Yvonne Porcella
Modesto, California

Yo Yolanda

Silks, cottons, cotton blends, silk ribbon, metallic inks; hand painted, hand and machine quilted; 42 x 64 inches.

This quilt is based on my experience working at the archeological site of Dashur located south of Cairo, Egypt. The form of the mud brick pyramid was distorted by erosion, but underground, where I worked drawing the sarcophagi, the burial chambers were left intact. These mysterious chambers seemed haunted by the royal princesses who had intended to inhabit them for eternity. My interest lies in the nexus of the physical and spiritual, the known and the unknown, the found and the sought.

Julia E. Pfaff
Richmond, Virginia

#109, Why Have We Come Here?/Dashur

Hand-dyed and painted cotton, zinc plate intaglio printing; machine pieced, hand embroidered, hand and machine quilted; 84 x 61 inches.

90

Alison Schwabe
Shelley, Australia

Obiri

Hand-dyed commercial
fabrics; reverse appliquéd,
machine pieced, and
machine quilted, hand em-
broidered; 20 x 28 inches.

*A recurring theme in some of my quilts is the fascination
with man-made marks and patterns on natural surfaces.
In the Northern Territory, Australia, stands Obiri Rock,
surrounded by green. Rock overhangs protect ancient mark-
ings from annual torrential rains and fierce sunlight. The
visitor looks far out across the plains, and behind, sees far
back into history through painted images there. The gold
embroidery represents the value to us of all such legacies.*

The path to the Giant Pines is a hiking/skiing trail in Tahquamenon State Park in Michigan's Upper Peninsula. Here, I continue my work with layering by exploring the detritus of the forest floor. Ignoring organic shapes and relying on the grid for structure allowed me to fully explore the play of color, light, and texture, as well as what is revealed and what is concealed.

Barbara Bushey
Ypsilanti, Michigan

Path to the Giant Pines IV

Cotton, acetate, cheese-cloth, and polyester; dyed, painted, discharged, layered, and machine stitched; 13 x 26 inches.

92

Jan Myers-Newbury
Pittsburgh, Pennsylvania

Ophelia's Dream

100% cotton muslin tie-dyed with Procion fiber reactive dyes; machine pieced and machine quilted; 76 x 68 inches.

Ophelia's Dream *is the current omega of a year-long evolution in my work from the geometric to the organic. I have never been as excited about the potential of applying transparent color to fabric as I am now. I have always been interested in manipulating color to create luminosity and the illusion of depth, and more and more of this seems to be happening in the dyepot, less in the piecing. And the layering of color upon color in a single yard of cloth seems a perhaps not accidental metaphor for the portion of my life that has fed these 18 years of quiltmaking.*

Savannah Cloth *was inspired by African mud cloth from Bamako in Southern Mali and strip weaving from the Savannah lands of Western Africa. A combination of physical constraints (e.g. loom size) and aesthetic criteria (e.g. means of combining strips) leads to the unique relationship between individual pieces and the whole. In more than any other art form I have encountered, the pieces push the limits of maintaining an individual integrity while still working together as a whole.*

Suzan Friedland
San Francisco, California

Savannah Cloth
Linen and silk; machine pieced and quilted, hand painted, laced with linen twine; 59 x 79 inches.

94

Lisa Clark
Burnsville, North Carolina

Blood and Bone

Paint, paper, fabric,
thread, and ink; photo-
transfer, monoprint, hand
stitched and painted,
35 x 38 inches.

This piece is part of a series in which I am exploring the question, "What is it to be human?" Are we merely blood and bone? I am looking for spirit in the body through the physical. Feeling my blood as the source of life, finding its source at the heart, feeling bones as physical structures that remain as imprints after life.

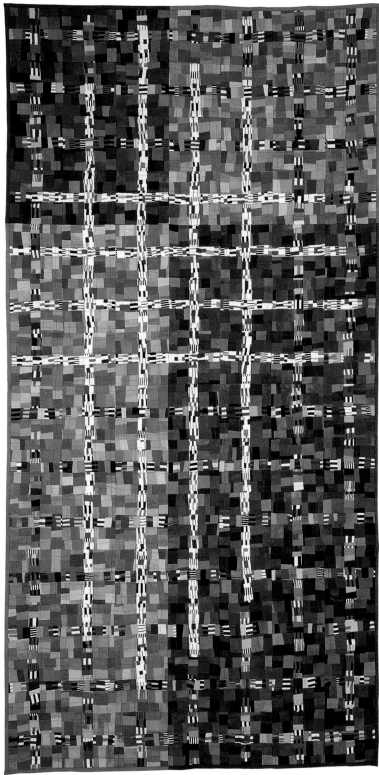

Overlay 1 is one of several quilts in which I have tried to present a grid composed of pieces varied in shape, pattern, color, and size, floating above an irregularly pieced background. I work with a method of curved strip piecing that introduces some unpredictability into my quilting. Never knowing exactly what to expect as I bring the quilt together, I remain intrigued throughout the construction process.

Ruth Garrison
Tempe, Arizona

Overlay 1
Cotton fabrics, some hand dyed; machine pieced and machine quilted; 40 x 79 inches.

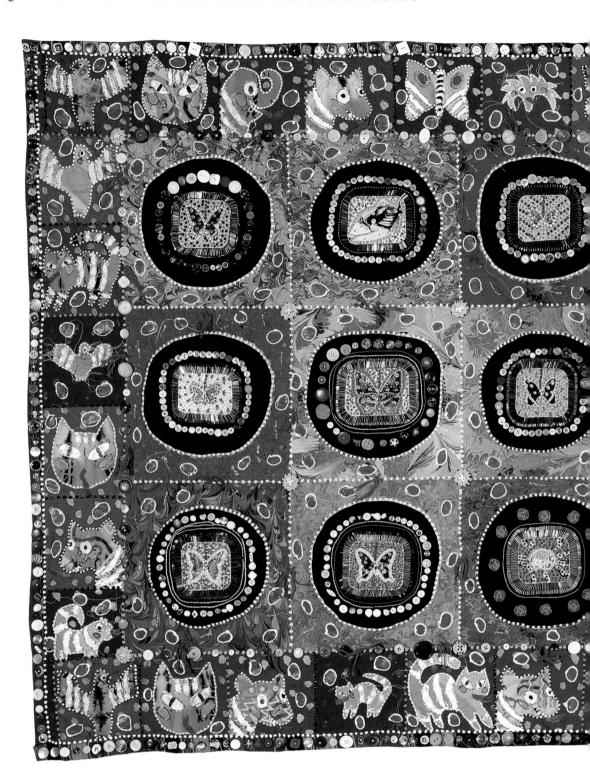

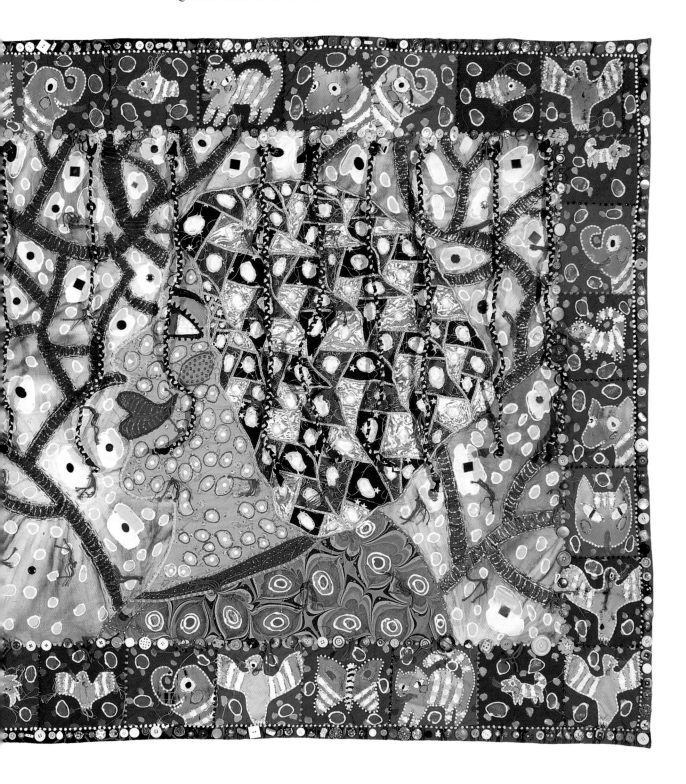

This quilt emerged as I thought about the traditional quilt versus the art quilt. Even though this quilt is based more on a painting concept, I wanted to express something about the beauty of the traditional quilt and the idea of sewing squares together.

Therese May
San Jose, California

**Contemplating
The Nine Patch**

Painted panels on mat board; hand quilted and tied, embellished with paint, beads and buttons; 90 x 50 inches. Courtesy of Mobilia Gallery.

98

Emily Richardson
Philadelphia, Pennsylvania

Night Clock

Textile paint on silk and
cotton, nylon net, silk
suture thread, and cotton
embroidery floss; direct
and reverse hand
appliquéd and embroi-
dered; hand quilted;
60 x 82 inches.

Night Clock *is a bed-size quilt made from painted strips of
sheer and lightweight fabrics, woven together in a way that
suggests dreams and thoughts weaving through a mind as it
sleeps: transparent, merging and dividing, creating and
altering time.* Night Clock *measures the unbalanced hours
of our sleep — forward, backward, lingering on one thing,
leaping to another, indifferent to any time but its own.*

*I came to understand the great strength and comfort of
quilts by learning to make them from women who <u>knew</u>:
knew the determination required by a project so complex;
knew and accepted the pain of fingers that quilt (no cry-
babies); knew how each quilt marks, not time, but our lives
— secrets shared or sewn into each piece, events which,
for Everywoman, become a record of her life.
This work pays homage to my sisters.*

Janice Fassinger
Cambridge, Ohio

**Our Lives —
Our Work**

Wool felt and photos;
knotted; 34 x 40 inches.

100

Hollis Chatelain
Bamako, Mali

Changes

Commercial fabrics printed
in Mali, Western Africa;
machine pieced, hand quilted, and then hand painted;
90 x 67 inches.

The beauty and contrast of Africa influence me in everyday
life. This quilt is the starting point of my evolution from
African prints to colored fabrics (that I also paint).
Extensive use of the prints taught me how to use bold colors.
Changes *has also helped me to discover my own style.*

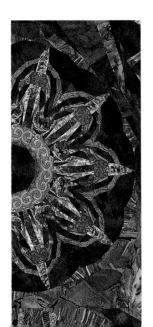

Kaleidoscope: the very word promises surprise and magic, change and chance. In choosing fabrics, I seek a random quality to imitate the chance interlinkings and endless possibilities synonymous with kaleidoscopes. The notion that there isn't an absolute or best selection is liberating. After all, a breathtaking collision of color in a scope's interior will maneuver into something different, something slightly new, during even the instant it takes to hand it to you.

Paula Nadelstern
Bronx, New York

**Kaleidoscopic XIII:
Random Acts of Color**

Cottons and blends; machine pieced and hand quilted; 59 x 56 inches.

102

Midge Hoffmann
Coburg, Oregon

Cosmic Garden

Silk Duppionne that has
been painted, stamped,
and stenciled; fused and
machine quilted;
25 x 35 inches.

*Design, pure color, and pattern are my passions. This piece
is the first I have produced with a method new to me —
painting silk, cutting, fusing, and random machine stitching.
This method suits me. It is quick and spontaneous, painterly
with a sense of quiltness. This work reflects the interconnectedness of life and matter throughout the universe. Stars,
planets, and comets are growing in this garden.*

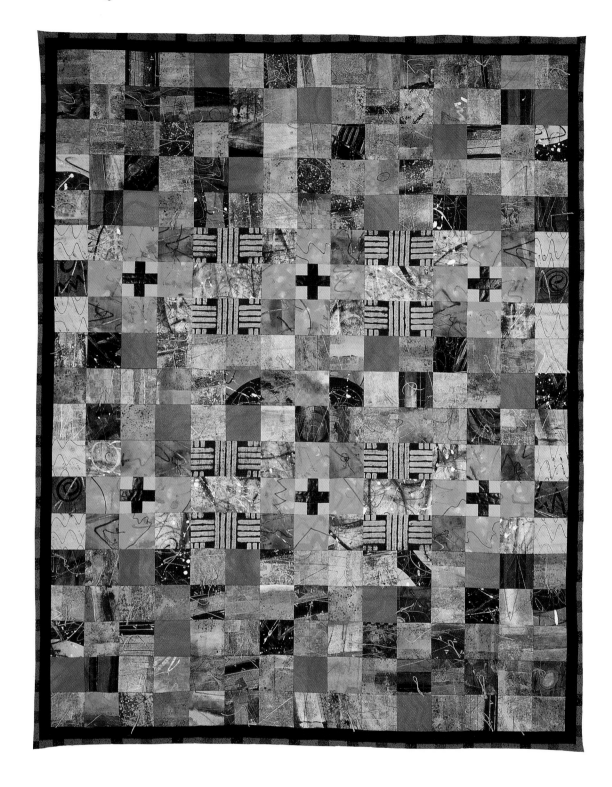

The Pecos National Monument sits on a low mesa amidst a magnificent landscape in the Southwest. Having visited this splendid Pueblo ruin with its two mission churches, kivas, and multiple domed adobes, one can only imagine life between A.D. 1450 and 1838 for the Native Americans and the Spanish conquerors.

Mary Allen Chaisson
South Harpswell, Maine

Pecos

Indonesian batik and assorted commercial cottons and blends that have been hand painted, dyed, and stamped; machine pieced and hand tied; 46 x 58 inches.

104

Jane A. Sassaman
Chicago, Illinois

Overgrown Garden
Commercial and hand-
stencilled cotton fabrics;
machine appliquéd and
machine quilted;
27 x 41 inches.

Overgrown Garden *attempts to capture the inex-*
haustible vitality of nature. This garden is organized
but has become a gloriously undisciplined field of energy,
each flower contributing its glory to the overall radiant
effect. We are all flowers in the garden.

Sometimes a new work knows what it wants to become and dictates its own transformation. Naive Art, our first collaboration, is such a quilt. After spontaneously cutting and piecing fabrics, Marilyn developed this small stitchery that has a primitive folk art quality. In order to give the small piece integrity, Herb constructed and beautifully carved the frame. The completed work seems warm and friendly — happy that it came into being.

Marilyn and
Herb Dillard
Longmont, Colorado

Naive Art

Cotton fabrics; machine
pieced, hand quilted, and
embroidered; aspen wood
frame, chip carved and
painted, embellished with
map tacks; 40 x 37 inches.

Two ideas came together at the inception of the "Sink or Swim" series. I had recently given birth to my first son and found myself alternately floating and sinking in a sea of motherhood. Also, my dye-painted silks began to remind me of underwater environments. Later in the series, as I gained confidence, I added elements of tropical fish. After the birth of my second son, I am still swimming.

Sue Benner
Dallas, Texas

Sink or Swim #21 & #22

Commercial silks treated with dyes; fused and machine quilted; 61 x 35 inches.

The Dairy Barn Cultural Arts Center, a unique arts facility located in the Appalachian foothills of southeastern Ohio, has been showcasing the finest regional, national, and international arts since 1978.

Harriet and Ora Anderson, long-time champions of the arts, worked with others in the community to establish a cultural arts center in a soon-to-be-demolished diary barn just minutes from Ohio University and the center of Athens. Through their efforts, the historic building was saved, and the Dairy Barn Southeastern Ohio Cultural Arts Center, a nonprofit corporation, was born.

Listed on the National Register of Historic Places, the Dairy Barn is now a state-of-the-art, handicapped-accessible facility that features a 7,000-square-foot gallery.

The Dairy Barn Cultural Arts Center is the site of festivals and events; invitational exhibitions of work by community artists; regional, national and international juried exhibitions; and a host of educational programs and activities for all ages. To the international community the Dairy Barn is best known for exhibitions and touring exhibits such as Quilt National, The Illustrator's Art and Contemporary Works in Wood.

The Dairy Barn is supported by admissions, memberships, corporate sponsorships, grants, and donations. The staff is assisted by a large group of volunteers who donate thousands of hours annually. For a Calendar of Events and information about other Dairy Barn programs contact the Dairy Barn Arts Center, P.O. Box 747, Athens, Ohio 45701.

The complete Quilt National '95 collection will be on display from May 27 through September 4, 1995 at the Dairy Barn Southeastern Ohio Cultural Arts Center, 8000 Dairy Lane, Athens, Ohio. Three separate collections of Quilt National '95 works will then begin a two-year tour of museums and galleries throughout the country. Most host venues will display only a portion of the full Quilt National '95 collection.

Tentative dates (unless otherwise noted) and locations are listed below. For an updated itinerary or to receive additional information about hosting a Quilt National touring collection, contact the Dairy Barn Cultural Arts Center, Post Office Box 747, Athens, Ohio, 45701-0747. Phone: 614-592-4981. FAX: 614-592-5090.

Date	Place
September 29 through October 1, 1995	Peoria, IL; Quilts Across America; site to be announced
October 1 through November 1, 1995	St. Louis, MO; Women's Center Self Help Benefit; site to be announced
October 28 through November 5, 1995	Houston, TX; International Quilt Festival; George Brown Convention Center
December 3, 1995 through January 14, 1996	Parkersburg, WV; Parkersburg Art Center (A)
January 13 through March 9, 1996	Pueblo, CO; Sangre de Cristo Arts and Conference Center (C)*
February 18 through March 31, 1996	Brockton, MA; Fuller Museum of Art (A)*
May, 1996	Bloomingdale, IL; Bloomingdale Park District (B)
August through October, 1996	Cincinnati, OH; Aronoff Center for the Arts
November 9, 1996 through January 4, 1997	Columbus, OH; Riffe Gallery (C)*
May, 1997	Bloomingdale, IL; Bloomingdale Park District (A)
June 15 through July 15, 1997	Oxford, OH; Miami University Museum

*Indicates a confirmed tour booking

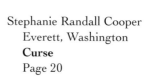

110

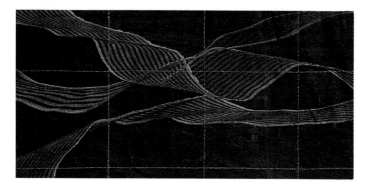

Above: Detail. Michael Mrowka.
See page 58.

Left: Detail. Elizabeth A. Busch. See page 44.

Right: Detail. Melody Johnson. See page 30.

111

112

Detail. Stephanie Randall Cooper. See page 20.